Paganism

Thorsons First Directions

Paganism

Vivianne Crowley

Thorsons
An Imprint of HarperCollinsPublishers
77–85 Fulham Palace Road
Hammersmith, London W6 8JB

Published by Thorsons 2000
10 9 8 7 6 5 4 3 2 1

Text copyright © Vivianne Crowley 2000
Copyright © Thorsons 2000

Editor: Jillian Stewart
Design: Wheelhouse Creative
Photography by Henry Allen, PhotoDisc Europe Ltd. and Images Colour Library

Text derived from *Principles of Paganism*
published by Thorsons 1996

Vivianne Crowley asserts the moral right to
be identified as the author of this work

A catalogue record for this book
is available from the British Library

ISBN 0 00 710334 4

Printed and bound in Hong Kong

Contents

Paganism

is the worship of the ancient pre-Christian

gods of our ancestors and of our lands

To those who walk the Ancient Pathways:

the Blessings of Earth and Sky,

of Moon and Sun.

What is Paganism?

Paganism is one of the fastest growing spiritual movements in the West today. Originally, the word 'Pagan' was applied to those who worshipped the Gods of the pagus, which in Latin means 'locality'. Pagan was also used in another sense by Christians – to mean 'country-dweller'. 'Heathen', of German origin, is also used by those who worship the Northern European Gods. Heathen means someone of the heath who worships the Gods of the land. In the West, the terms Native Spirituality, Celtic Spirituality, European Traditional Religion, the Elder Faith and the Old Religion are also used to describe the Pagan religions.

Pagans today

To be Pagan is to worship the ancient pre-Christian Gods of our ancestors and of our lands. This idea may seem strange in our modern world. Why do Pagans worship these ancient and dusty images? We worship our Gods because they are not forgotten archaeological artefacts but living energies of great power. They have endured in the group memory of humanity, the collective unconscious, which is the storehouse of all our religious longing and experience.

Pagan religion is based on teachings handed down through myth and saga over thousands of years. Paganism has never died. Instead our ancient Pagan beliefs have been seen as merely myth or fairy stories which have no relevance today. However, the fact that we cherish and pass on these myths shows that they do have relevance. The myths have survived because they speak to us in the language of dream, symbol and allegory. They tease the conscious mind because we do not fully understand them; yet we know beneath their symbolism are undying truths. They are important because they contain the spiritual wisdom not of one individual, but of many people over great periods of time. They are the living breathing dreams of the Gods, sent to show us the way to our true destiny, which is to rest once more in unity and

harmony with the Divine forces of Heaven and Earth.

Pagan religion is all around us – in the landscape moulded by generations before into sacred hill and standing stone, into sacred burial ground and holy mountain, places where generations have walked, honouring their Gods. It is a religion preserved in folk song and dance and in seasonal custom. We weave our corn dollies, we bob for apples at Hallowe'en, not remembering that these are the remnants of the religious celebrations of our ancestors the Celts, the Germani and the other tribes who make up our Western inheritance.

As we enter the new millennium, we are seeing a rebirth of ancient spiritual traditions. People all over the world are rejecting newer religions and returning to the wisdom of their ancestors.

Some worshippers of the Pagan Gods describe themselves simply as Pagans, Heathens, Goddess worshippers or members of the Old Religion. Others follow particular traditions within Paganism. One of the most well known is Druidry or Druidism – the Druids were the priesthood of the Celts and great poets and healers. Others described themselves as Odinists – followers of Odin, or Asatru, followers of the High Gods of North Europe of whom Odin is chief. Others say they are followers of WiseCraft or Witchcraft. This is not the Witchcraft of Black Masses and Devil-worship, but the true WiseCraft of the land, which honours the Gods and practises magic, healing crafts and the sight – those latent psychic abilities within us all which recent centuries have sought to suppress. Some call themselves Wiccan, a form of WiseCraft that honours the Great Mother Goddess and Horned God but also draws its inspiration from the Mystery Religions of the ancient world which taught our ancestors the way to self-knowledge and knowledge of the Gods. Other Pagans practise the Mysteries of the ancient Greeks or of Mithras, the Sun God of the Roman soldiery. In North America, many turn for inspiration to Native American spirituality, perhaps because they have Native American ancestry and feel a need to return to their ancient heritage, or because this spirituality is rooted in the land to which their ancestors emigrated.

Although the forms in which the Gods are worshipped vary, there is sufficient commonality for them all to recognize themselves as part of the growing spiritual movement that is Paganism.

Pagan Beliefs

Pagans have a variety of beliefs, but at their core are three which many would share:

- The Divine has made Itself manifest through many Deities in different places and at different times. No one Deity can express the totality of the Divine. This can be called *polytheism* – the Gods are many.
- The Divine is present in Nature and in each one of us. This can be called *pantheism* – the Divine is everywhere.
- Goddess and God: The Divine is represented as both female (Goddess) and male (God) while understanding that It is beyond the limitations of gender.

Polytheism

It has been easy in the past for the simple to believe that their version of religion was right, true, self-evidently good, the only acceptable truth and that people of other languages and races who held different beliefs were primitive, wrong-headed, misguided or simply evil. Paganism does *not* teach that there is only one right way to worship the Divine or that the teachings of one particular racial group are superior to another. We do not seek to *export* our religions and foist them on others through force, bribery or fear. Polytheism means that we can respect the Gods of others and recognize in them another beauteous manifestation of the Divine force. The various Pagan polytheisms are therefore religions of tolerance.

Pagans worship the ancient Gods, but we are not harking back to a romantic past. We believe that in the past and in our ancient Gods lie keys to understanding the future. We also believe that human society is like a tree. It cannot live in mid-air. It must be rooted in the Earth and the Gods of the Earth and it must be rooted in an understanding of the past – both its wisdom and its mistakes.

Another besetting folly of humankind is to think the world is static and unchanging. All scientific evidence is to the contrary – time and change march on, the seasonal cycle turns and turns again, we age. Yet always we wish to stop the passage of time. We cling to that which is outworn and has lost its usefulness; but to cling to stasis is to cling to illusion, for the message of the cosmos is change.

The law of change means that our religious forms and visions must evolve as society evolves and changes. New situations create new spiritual needs. The Pagan traditions are not religions whose teachings are engraved on tablets of stone.

Pantheism

Paganism venerates the force of life itself, which is continually unfolding, renewing, disintegrating, returning to its source, resting and then awakening and renewing again. Many Pagans believe in a conscious and creative universe in which humans and the rest of creation are the eyes and ears, the brain and hands. All our experience is fed into the group mind of humanity which in turn feeds the consciousness of the universe.

To Pagans, it is important to remember and honour the force which gives rise to us and sustains us. Life and consciousness are precious gifts and so too is the natural world of which we are a part. The Divine is like the breath of the universe that gives rise to the force of life itself. The Divine is within the air we breathe, the water we drink, the human, animal and plant life all around us. Just as we are spirits who inhabit a body, so too does the Divine inhabit the universe around us. These pantheistic beliefs – that the Divine is in Nature – were natural to our ancestors for whom nature was an intimate part of their lives.

Today, for many of us Nature seems remote and devoid of spirit. Our hearts no longer give thanks to the Goddess when the flowers bloom, when our crops thrive. We give thanks to weed killer and phosphates!

Unfortunately, this so-called rational rather than reverential attitude to Nature is disastrous for our future. We are encouraged to exploit Nature and to overturn her balance, to cut down and burn precious resources, alter our seasons, suspend our rainfall and believe that we are *making progress* even as we are sinking into the grossest stupidity.

This may suggest that Paganism is advocating a return to a romantic eco-friendly past, but Paganism is a practical religion concerned with the problems of the present. It is a green religion. It encourages us to live in love and kinship with the natural world. The world was not created by the Gods for our benefit. We are part of Nature – cells in a functioning whole. Instead of perceiving the universe to be anthropocentric and available to be exploited to meet the needs of human beings, Paganism sees it as holistic and having its own purposes in which human beings play only a part.

Goddess and God

The oppression of Nature has been mirrored by other forms of oppression, notably that of spirituality, philosophy and society of the feminine. The newer religions of the past two millennia are based on a fundamental error: that the Divine can be depicted as solely male. This is a nonsensical belief if only we stop to think about it. The Divine has manifested over the ages as both Goddess and God to help us understand Its manifold complexity. If we worship only half of the Divine, then understanding will be lost. We disenfranchise half of our fellows.

Paganism teaches that both women and men, girls and boys, Goddess and God are equally valuable and necessary to a balanced and whole society and creation. Paganism teaches that to be a whole man is to be strong, loving, generous, gentle and nurturing. It does not imprison us in a strait-jacket of sexually stereotyped behaviour that denies on the one hand to women their power to interact in the world and on the other to men the power to express love and caring.

The past millennium in the West has been dominated by a Christian ethos which has had very negative attitudes to sex, particularly in relation to women. In Paganism, however, the body is considered the temple of the Divine spark within us. Our senses relay to us the beauties of the physical world, which is a manifestation of the Divine force. Nature is therefore good and so too is the physical realm. Union with the Divine is to be sought in the material world, not only in the spiritual realm beyond. The body need not be a distraction from spirituality.

Pagan ethics

Paganism does not have a complex set of commandments, but teaches that we must examine our conduct in the light of a simple meta-rule: if it harms none, it is permissible. We must ask ourselves, 'What impact will my actions have on others? Will they cause hurt or harm? Can I do this, take this, say this without damage to other human beings, other species, the planet itself?' This is the way of *least harm*.

Pagans recognize that the very existence of the human race is a threat to the rest of the planet's creation. We are greedy for resources, we exploit other species and give little in return. Yet exist we do and our continued existence lies in ensuring that we steer our society towards those values that are likely to preserve not only the human race but also the planet around us.

Giving something back to the Earth in return for the life she gives us is important in Paganism and is found throughout Pagan thought. One old Pagan prayer from Lithuania (one of the last countries in Europe to be Christianized) speaks of planting trees of thanks. We may feel that such a contribution is very small, but we can not only do something ourselves, we can encourage others to do the same.

Conserving Nature means preserving the beautiful diversity with which our Gods have seen fit to furnish us. We do not yet understand the complex interaction of our biosphere and the role which each life form has to play in its maintenance. We meddle with this balance at our peril. Active Pagans are therefore involved not only in land conservation but also in animal conservation and animal rights.

Pagans believe that the way society today teaches us to relate to one another is in many ways wrong. We are taught a rampant, 'me first' individualism. We are taught to consume as much as possible without thought of the consequences for others, both now and in the future. This is because we have lost the ties of kinship and clan which once bound us to other people. We live in a world which is the most densely populated it has ever been, but many of whose people are alienated, isolated and lonely. Paganism teaches that we are not separate and alone – we are each plants from a common root. Our connectedness means that mutual help and aid are important in Paganism.

Balance and harmony

'Balance' and 'harmony' are key words in Paganism. No quality in excess is good. We must learn to use each quality skilfully in its own due place. Inevitably at times, we will fail. All of us get things wrong. Having done so, we must forgive ourselves and start again. To start again, we must seek to redress the balance by contributing positive energy and action where we have contributed negative.

One way of helping us live a balanced and harmonious life is to practise honour and truth. These are important concepts in Paganism. By keeping our word, our honour and our truth we help to evolve humanity as a whole.

To live a balanced life we must also consider the way in which we live. 'Right livelihood' is a Buddhist phrase, but one that is equally applicable to Pagans. Obviously, one Pagan's definition of right livelihood may not be the same as another's, but we must each examine and question our motives and the morality of what we do, often in the light of the meta-principle of: what will contribute to the greater good?

Life and death

Paganism differs from many religions in its attitude to life and death. Since Nature is a manifestation of the Divine and life on Earth is a pleasure and a gift, then we can be in union with the Divine in this life as well as in the one beyond. The Pagan ethos focuses on enjoying and celebrating the fact of life itself and the gift of consciousness.

Life is balanced by death. What do Pagans believe about death? Most Pagan traditions teach reincarnation: our life on Earth is one of many and the purpose of life is to learn and evolve. Some Pagans have ideas similar to Hindus about karma: our lives are affected by the implications of our past actions. Others believe that although the life force and that spark within us which is part of it endure, transform and live again, the slate is washed clean and we do not carry the past forward with us.

Not all Pagans believe that they as individuals will live again. Many believe that their life essence is undying and will reform into new life, but this is more in the nature of material which is broken down and reused. They do not expect to remember previous incarnations but see each life experience as unique.

Is Paganism Appropriate to Me?

One of the most obvious things which strikes anyone who goes to a Pagan gathering is the diversity of the Pagan community. Walking around Avebury stone circle once with a Pagan group from London, I was surprised to notice that everyone was looking at us. Turning round to look at our party wending its way around the stones, I could see why. It was not that any one individual looked unusual, but it was the combination of elderly English ladies with walking sticks, middle-aged men in sports jackets, leather-jacketed Goths with pierced noses, families carrying babies, hippies whose dress style hadn't changed since 1972, men with pony tails, men and women with hennaed hair or shaven heads … Yes, collectively, we were an unusual group.

Pagans come from all walks of life and all age groups.

The Pagan movement began to grow enormously from the 1970s onwards. This might mean that it is primarily a young movement, but this is not the case. People tend to look at spirituality during periods in their lives when they have most time to think about themselves and where they are going. This may be when they are bringing up young children and have to teach them ethics and a spiritual framework in which to set them. This can be the time when they realize that their own spiritual life is deficient and that they need to do something about it. Often, however, people examine their spirituality either when they are young or else from middle age onwards, when they have more free time to indulge in such luxuries. Many people become Pagans in their twenties; many become Pagans in their forties, fifties or later.

How do people come to Paganism?

Many of us grow up with a sense that Nature is sacred and Divine. It is natural for children to make altars in the woods and to honour the spirits of the trees, in the same way that children everywhere make sand castles upon the beach. We do not need to be taught these things, though some of us are. As we grow up, many of us forget the sense of sacred presence in tree or stream or by the sea, but some do not. Many of us find that we turn our prayers spontaneously to the Goddess or to the Great Spirit; that the Gods we find in our city temples and churches are not the Gods that speak to us in our dreams and visions.

If we are Celts, perhaps we read the myths of our Celtic Deities – if we are Native American, perhaps we read of the ancient ways of our grandfathers and grandmothers – and found that these myths and legends spoke to us with a power and resonance which the religion we were taught as children lacked.

There may be clues that led us to discover that we are not strange or otherworldly or bound up in a forgotten past, but that we are Pagans. We may have read a book about modern Paganism, heard a radio interview, read a magazine article, or met someone through work or college who said, 'I am a Pagan,' and we knew then that we were too.

Finding a path

Paganism teaches that we are each responsible for ourselves. This means we must take responsibility for our own spiritual development. Others who travel the same path may offer us wisdom and advice, and particular Pagan traditions can sustain and help us, but in the end we must become our own teachers and guides.

Paganism does not have a central controlling body. There are, however, a number of Pagan organizations, staffed primarily by volunteers, which serve as information giving and networking bodies (some of these are listed at the end of this book). There are also large organizations representing groups following particular Pagan paths such as

Druidry, Wicca, Odinism/Asatru or the Paganism of particular ethnic communities.

No one, however, needs to join a Pagan organization to become a Pagan, though many do. Often we want to meet with others to celebrate and worship together and to learn and share ideas. However, we need no ceremony and we need not be 'saved', for there is nothing to be saved from. We need only to commit ourselves earnestly in our hearts to the ancient Deities of our lands and peoples.

This then is how some people come to Paganism, but who and what do Pagans worship?

The Pagan Gods

Our ancestors honoured Nature in her many manifestations because they had a deep and intimate relationship with the natural landscape. It is easy to imagine how certain places came to be seen as sacred and how we came to worship the Deities of distinctive natural features such as rocks, trees, mountains, lakes, rivers or springs. Our original Gods belonged often to specific places.

Other Gods belonged to specific tribes. Nomadic peoples, who were hunters and later herders, needed portable Gods. Each tribe or clan had its own presiding Deity who guarded and protected his or her people. Certain important human activities also came to have their own presiding Deities who initiated their worshippers into the mysteries of their arts. Sometimes Deities had more than one function. Sometimes a function had more than one Deity. Thus did the Gods and Goddesses multiply and our ancestors were polytheists – worshippers of many Deities.

The question is: why do we need Gods at all? Why do we not just say that the Divine is abstract? Unfortunately, the human mind, for most of us anyway, does not think in abstractions. Thus the beautiful forms of the Gods which our ancestors have worshipped over the ages still have the power to move us, inspire us, stretch our minds. We know that each image by itself is limited, but if we honour the many Gods in our minds, our hearts and our spirit, they will bring us to a true understanding: that the Divine is present within us and without us, in all times and places, ever-changing, ever the same.

Modern Paganism and ancient Gods

Some modern Pagans have a devotion to a particular Goddess or God; others choose to venerate the Divine through the Gods and Goddesses of one particular pantheon. Often, however, Pagans honour the Gods under a number of different names. This can seem somewhat bewildering but it is perhaps less so if the Gods are thought of as different personalities through which the Divine has chosen to manifest Itself at different times and to different peoples.

Today, Pagans worship the Divine as Goddess, God and also as the Great Spirit or One who is beyond all these. Some Pagans honour the Gods in their Norse form, others in Celtic form, Egyptian form or according to the ways of Native American ancestors. A distinctive feature of Paganism, however, is the emphasis it places on the Divine in female form – the Goddess.

Goddess

In whatever Pagan pantheon we look, we find strong and powerful
Goddess figures, queens in their own right, Mistresses of the worlds
of Magic, the Otherworld and the everyday world of women and men.
Above all, we have in the Goddess the image of the loving mother, who
provides for us, cherishes us, who gives us rest when we are weary,
food when we are hungry, healing when we are in pain, and who with
her last breath protects us. Many modern Pagans speak of 'The
Goddess', meaning the essence behind all the different Goddesses
who have been worshipped all over the world. A chant which is
often heard at Pagan gatherings sings to the Goddess as:

Isis, Astarte, Diana, Hecate, Demeter, Kali, Inanna

These many names from the past are seen as representing different
aspects of the Great Goddess who is universal and present in all
cultures and at all times, the eternal feminine, the Divine She.

The Triple Goddess

One concept of the Goddess which is found in ancient Paganism but which is more widespread in modern Paganism is that of the Triple Goddess – the Goddess as a triplicity of Virgin, Mother and Crone, often symbolized by the Waxing, Full and Waning Moons.

One reason for the popularity of the Triple Goddess is that She represents all aspects of the female life-cycle – the freedom and independence of youth, the joys and the sorrows of motherhood, and the wisdom and independence which return when we are free of the obligations of family. In Paganism the Virgin aspect of the Goddess is not necessarily Virgin in the sense of non-sexual, but Virgin in the sense of not owned by a husband. The Mother aspect of the Triple Goddess is represented by the Full Moon. She is also represented by the Earth. Often this aspect of the Goddess is seen as Gaia, the Earth itself, and is thought of as The Great Mother – the Divinity which gives birth to us, nourishes us, sustains us, and in which we finally find our rest and rebirth.

The Triple Goddess is also honoured as Wise Woman, Crone or Hag, the keeper of the mysteries. For a woman, the Crone Goddess symbolizes her own inner wisdom.

Virgin Goddesses

Diana and Aradia

Two Roman Goddesses who play an important role in women's Paganism and in WiseCraft are the Moon Goddess Diana and her daughter Aradia. One branch of WiseCraft – the Dianic Craft, which is primarily for women – is dedicated to Diana. Despite her role as Virgin Goddess, Diana presided over childbirth and could bless women with children.

Aradia is the Italian version of the name of the Classical Goddess Herodias, whom some medieval texts claim was widely worshipped across Southern Europe into medieval times.

Aradia and her mother Diana are described as saviour Goddesses of the peasants against their oppressive feudal lords and could be appealed to for help in all of life's problems.

Mother Goddess

Isis

Isis is an Egyptian Mother Goddess who was widely worshipped throughout Egyptian history. She was the sister of Osiris, the God of Death and Resurrection, and mother of the God Horus. One of the largest Goddess-worshipping movements in the Western world today is the Fellowship of Isis.

Isis became widely known following Alexander the Great's conquest of Egypt about 2,000 years ago. Greek followers of Alexander took over as rulers of Egypt and were anxious to integrate themselves with Egyptian society. To provide a unifying religion, a small number of Deities were 'promoted' to being chief Gods of Egypt and a focus of worship for Egyptian and Greek alike. The most popular Deity was Isis.

Then the Romans, finding the religions offered by the state unsatisfying, looked elsewhere. They were as fascinated with the East as the many spiritual seekers who headed East in the nineteenth and twentieth centuries, so by the time of Julius Caesar, a temple of Isis had been established in Rome on the Capitoline Hill. It lasted for four centuries. For many, Isis became *the* Goddess.

Crone Goddesses

Hecate, Morrigan, Cerridwen

Hecate

A Greek Moon Goddess and Goddess of Witchery, Hecate is worshipped both in WiseCraft and by women's groups. Sender of nocturnal visions, her rites were often performed at night – as is fitting for a Moon Goddess. She was particularly associated with cross-roads, which have always been thought of as places transformation.

In Greece her main festival was at the August harvest – the equivalent of the Lammas harvest celebration in Western Paganism. Hecate was associated with the Moon and the Moon with rain, for the weather often changes at the New and Full Moons. She was therefore seen as having control over the weather and her aid was invoked to help avert storms which might damage the August harvest.

Morrigan

The Morrigan is venerated in Celtic traditions of WiseCraft and in Druidry. In Celtic mythology, she is the fearsome and powerful Triple Goddess of Battle and Death, who appears in her three forms of

Morrigan, Badhbh and Nemhain. Her symbol is the raven, which is perhaps not surprising, given that ravens feast on the bodies of the dead after battle.

Cerridwen

Another Celtic Deity whose name is widely used in Druidry and WiseCraft is the Welsh Goddess Cerridwen. Like Hecate, she is associated with magic and the Crone aspect of the Goddess, the Waning Moon. A popular Goddess chant is:

Hecate, Cerridwen, Dark Mother, take us in
Hecate, Cerridwen, let us be reborn

Why should there be so much interest in these superficially less attractive aspects of the Goddess? Cerridwen is a Goddess of transformation and hence initiation. Many people coming to Paganism today are seeking inner wisdom and transformation, teachings which were once the province of the ancient Pagan mystery schools. Cerridwen is also is the keeper of hidden wisdom and although fearsome as Hag and pursuer, yet offers those who walk her ways insight into the depths of their soul and being.

Star Goddess

Arianrhod

Arianrhod is another Welsh Goddess and is invoked often in WiseCraft and Druidry. Her names means 'Silver Wheel' and she is the mother of Lleu Llaw Gyffes, the Welsh equivalent of the Irish God Lugh.

Caer Arianrhod, the Castle of Arianrhod, is placed in the Northern heavens and Arianrhod is associated with the pole-star. Caer Arianrhod is considered particularly sacred in some traditions of WiseCraft as the shining beacon which guides our spiritual destiny.

Fire Goddess

Bride

The Irish Goddess Brigit, Brigid or Bride (pronounced B*reed*), patron of artists, smiths and healers, is honoured in Druidry and WiseCraft. Bride was the daughter of the *Dagda* or Good God, the principal God of the Irish race known as the *Tuatha dé Danaan*, People of Dana, Dana being the Mother Goddess.

Brigit was often depicted as a Triple Goddess. Her chief shrine was in

Kildare, where her vigil fire was tended by unmarried priestesses known as *Inghean an Dagha*, Daughters of Fire. When Ireland succumbed to Christianization, Brigid became St Brigid and her shrine was taken over by nuns.

Rhiannon

In Welsh myth, one of the most important Goddesses is Rhiannon. Scholars have suggested that her name means 'Great Queen'. Some believe she is the same horse Goddess who was venerated on Continental Europe as Epona. Epona was hailed as Regina, Queen, by her Roman followers and was worshipped by Celt and Roman alike during the time of the Roman Empire.

Freya

Freya is honoured today by Pagans of the Northern Tradition and also in Northern European Wicca. She and Odin are the most frequently mentioned Deities in German medieval texts.

Freya is a Goddess of Love, Beauty and Fertility, but half of the battle-slain are also hers. Riding across the battlefields with the Valkyrie warrior women, she makes her choice. Those who do not go to Freya's feasting hall go to that of Odin. Freya is married to Odur, whose name is so similar to that of Odin that many consider Freya and Frigga, Odin's wife, to be the same Goddess. Freya is also a patroness of magic and was renowned for her sexual liaisons.

Frigga

Frigga is the Mother of the Gods and Goddess of the Sky. She has the power to see the future. She is a patroness of marriage and fertility, and her health was always toasted at wedding feasts. She was also called upon by women in labour. Despite her domestic traits, Frigga's imagery is bound up with that of the medieval witch. A picture of Frigga naked riding a distaff which looks much like a broomstick can be found on the wall of Schleswig cathedral in North Germany. This image is from the twelfth century, which suggests that at that period Goddess worship had not succumbed entirely to Christianity.

God

Modern Paganism has many Gods, who, like its Goddesses, are drawn from a number of different pantheons. Unlike many other religions, in Paganism, the God is conceived of as operating within Nature. Pagan God images are both animalistic and sexual. They recognize human beings in totality – that is, that we are creatures of primitive biological instinct, of human love and caring, and of spiritual longings and aspirations.

As with the Goddess, particular aspects of the Pagan Gods have risen to prominence in modern Paganism in order to meet the needs of Pagans today. Two of the most common aspects of the God are the Horned God and the Green Man. Both reflect modern Paganism's concern with maintaining our planet and our natural environment. They are also a recognition that we can live fulfilled and whole lives only if we acknowledge ourselves as part of Nature, not separate from it.

The Horned God

The Horned and phallic God is an image found in many Pagan cultures. As Pan he was venerated by the Greeks. To the Celts he was Cernunnos or Herne, names which derive from the word 'horn'.

Cernunnos' sacred animal is the stag and it is primarily as Stag God that the Horned God is honoured by Pagans today. His body is that of a man, but his feet are hooves and his antlers reach up to heaven, capturing within them the power of the Sun. The Pagan image of the Horned God has been much maligned in recent centuries by attempts to identify him with the Christian Devil, but modern Paganism has seen its rebirth and rehabilitation.

Why should this seemingly primitive and animalistic image hold such appeal? Many Pagans believe that the cerebral and celibate images of God which have prevailed in recent millennia are negative for both women and men. The implicit message – and often the explicit one – is that sexuality is wrong. The Christian God is a desexualized God, which creates problems in accommodating our sexual nature.

The Green Man

The Green Man is a very early form of Deity. Often he is found in conjunction with the Great Mother Goddess. He is both her son and her lover. She gives birth to him; he impregnates her; she sacrifices him and he is reborn. This was a way in which some of our ancestors symbolized the reappearance of green growth each spring and its disappearance in the autumn or fall.

The Green Man represents the return of fertility to the land after winter's bareness. He is therefore a phallic aspect of the God and a giver of plenty. In English folklore celebrations, the Green Man appears as a tall man dressed in leaves and carrying a staff. Indeed, many Pagans believe the stories of Robin Hood originated in Pagan myths of the Green Man of the forest.

Dagda

Aspects of the Green Man are found in the Irish God, the Dagda. The Dagda is the All-Father, *Eochaid Ollathair*, and is wise and knowledgeable. His weapon is a club and he also possesses a magical cauldron which can never be emptied. There are suggestions that the chalk image of a

giant phallic figure with a staff which is carved into the hillside at the village of Cerne (i.e. horn) Abbas in South West England is an image of the Dagda or his English equivalent.

Frey

In the Northern Tradition, there are aspects of both the Green Man and the Horned God in Frey, the chief God of the Vanir, whose name means 'Lord'. Frey and his twin sister the Goddess Freya are the children of the fertility Earth Goddess Nerthus and the Sea God Njörd. Frey is distinguished by his erect phallus and has similarities to other Nature Gods such as Cernunnos and Pan. The link with the Horned God appears when Frey fights Surt the destroyer with a pair of antlers, having given up his magical sword as part of a bride price.

Thor

Some aspects of the fertile, life-loving, Green Man aspect of the God are also found in the Northern Tradition in the form of the God Thor. Thor is associated with oak trees and we know that the German tribes most frequently worshipped their Gods in forest clearings. Thor was a 'people's God' and his concerns were agriculture as well as war.

Thor was described as Odin's son by the giantess Jord or Jorth, who represents the Earth. Thor shares the Dagda's strength but his weapon is a hammer, Mjolnir, which can slay giants and shatter rocks, rather than a club. The Romans associated Thor with Hercules, another mighty wielder of clubs. Thor is also a God of Lightning and was seen by the Romans as having many similarities to the Sky God Jupiter, to whom the oak was also sacred.

Odin

Another major form in which the God is worshipped in modern Paganism is as Odin, who is also known by his Anglo-Saxon name of Woden or Wotan. Wednesday in the English calendar was originally Wotan's Day.

Odin is a God of Wisdom, Knowledge and Communication and possesses not only knowledge of this world but also knowledge of the Otherworld. To gain this knowledge he must undergo many ordeals. In one such ordeal he sacrifices an eye in order to gain access to knowledge and thereafter was one-eyed. Odin also discovered the runes through a nine day ordeal in which he hung upside-down fasting on the World Tree. The runes are the letters of the Norse and German alphabets, but also much more. They can be used as a magical and divinatory system and are popular as such today. They are shuffled in a similar way to tarot cards and the yarrow stalks of the I *Ching* and the pattern into which they fall is a microcosm – a miniature reflection – of the patterning of events in the universe. The right chanting of the runes can also be used as a method of magic-making.

Gods of Light

In the Pagan calendar, there are many festivals when the God appears primarily in solar guise, either as a Sun King, Sun Child, the Child of Promise or the Light Bearer. These aspects of the God are associated primarily with the Winter and Summer Solstices, although the Celtic God Lugh is also associated with the August harvest festival of Lughnasadh (pronounced *Loonasa*).

Lugh

Lugh is an Irish Deity, the grandson of the healing God Dian Cécht.
Described as a young warrior of fair countenance, he was also a wise
man and a sorcerer. He is also known as God of the arts and crafts and
gained entry to the Hall of the High King of Ireland in Tara by claiming
to be able to do most of the recognized occupations in roughly
ascending order of prestige. First he claims to be a carpenter, then a
smith, champion, harper, hero, historian, magician, doctor and poet. As

there is no one else in Tara who can do all of these things, Lugh is admitted and becomes adviser to the king.

Balder

In the Northern Tradition, Balder is a God of Light and Radiance, whose brother is blind Hodur, the darkness. Balder and Hodur are the sons of Frigga and Odin. Odin engraves the runes upon Balder's tongue which gives him the power to sing the runes and so to perform magic. He is so beautiful and good that his appearance fills everyone with gladness. He is almost immortal, for there is only one thing in existence which can harm him: mistletoe.

It is Balder's half-brother Loki, known as the Wizard of Lies, who brings about his downfall. Loki tricks their mother Frigga into revealing that mistletoe can kill Balder. At Midwinter Solstice, Loki fashions a mistletoe dart and tricks Balder's brother, the blind Holdur, into throwing it. Balder is killed.

These are by no means all of the many different forms in which modern Pagans honour their Gods, but those described here give a glimpse of the richness of Pagan mythology. In the next chapter we will look at Pagan festivals and see how the different aspects of the Deities are honoured at different points of the seasonal cycle.

Celebrating the Seasonal Cycle

All religions have seasonal festivals which mark the calendar of the year. In countries where Christianity has been the dominant religion, many of the ideas and symbolism used have been borrowed from pre-Christian Paganism.

Most Pagans celebrate a seasonal cycle of eight festivals. Four of these are known by their Celtic names. The other four are related to the solar cycle – the Spring and Autumn or Fall Equinoxes, when the hours of daylight equal the hours of light; Summer Solstice, the longest day; and Winter Solstice, the longest night of the year. These eight festivals are spaced throughout the year, so there is a Pagan festival every six to seven weeks. The seasonal cycle is often called the Wheel of the Year.

Celebrating the festivals

This is a description of the seasonal cycle which is based on a temperate climate. Pagans, however, vary in the way in which they celebrate the festivals. Some variations are regional. In the far North, parts of Scandinavia and Canada for instance, the Spring Equinox is not an appropriate time to celebrate the sowing of seeds, as this must take place much later in the year in what is a very short agricultural season.

Different festivals are associated with different times of day. This does not mean we have to celebrate them at those times, but meditating on the symbolism of the timing will help us to understand the meaning of the festival.

The Wheel of the Year in the Northern Hemisphere

The Wheel of the Year in the Southern Hemisphere

Imbolc/Candlemas

(the hours before and up to dawn)

Life is renewing, the light is returning

Imbolc is an Irish word and originally it was thought to mean 'in the belly'. The festival is also sometimes known by its name in the Christian calendar, which is Candlemas – the feast of candles.

Imbolc is a festival which is dedicated both to the Goddess and to the return of light to the land. In many Pagan traditions, the Goddess is considered to be in the Underworld throughout the winter. Around Imbolc, the first signs of the passing of winter appear. The lengthening days awaken Nature. The first spring flowers appear – snowdrops, crocuses – sometimes emerging from the snow itself. We know that even if the land seems barren, the life force is awakening.

Our ancestors celebrated this festival with light. In Scandinavia, for instance, a young woman representing the Goddess was crowned with a crown of candles. Pagans today celebrate Imbolc in many ways. The Goddess may be invited to leave the Underworld and to return to the Middle World, the world of Nature. She can be invited by an invocation – a calling unto the Goddess. This may be by one person or by many.

One Goddess who is frequently invoked at Imbolc is the Celtic Goddess Brigid or Bride. As a Fire Goddess, she is appropriate to a festival which celebrates the return of the Sun and longer days. Imbolc is a time of purification. The windows are opened in our houses and in our minds to let in fresh air and thought. It is a time for new beginnings and for emerging out of winter hibernation to begin the work of the coming year.

Spring Equinox

(dawn)

The buds are unfurling, the Stag God is calling

By Spring Equinox, we know that the seasons are really changing and that the life force is renewing. Birds are singing and nest building, the buds on the trees are opening their light green leaves, the colour which signifies spring.

To the ancient Germans, this was the festival of the Goddess Ostara, whose name comes from the same root as the female hormone oestrogen. Ostara's symbol is an egg, a symbol which appears today in some countries in the form of chocolate Easter eggs and in others as green-painted eggs, symbolic of spring fertility. There are many traditional customs associated with eggs which form part of Pagan celebrations today. In some countries eggs are hidden around the house and garden for children to find. In others, hard-boiled eggs are rolled downhill, with the fastest egg winning the race. Whatever the custom, it reminds us of the importance of the renewal of the life force.

This is also the time in the agricultural calendar when seeds are sown in the ploughed fields and when the hours of darkness are equal to the hours of light. All these elements may be woven into Spring celebrations. Solitary Pagans may tend their gardens and contemplate with the sowing of seeds for the coming season the power and endurance of the life force.

While Imbolc is often a time to plan new projects, the Spring Equinox is a time to begin them. In Nature, birds have built their nests and now lay eggs. Astrologically, at Spring Equinox the Sun is considered to be in the sign of Aries. This is a sign of energy and activity. The plans and ideas we have formulated at Imbolc under the airy sign of Aquarius can now be given energy and life.

Beltane

(mid-morning)

The May Queen is crowned, and calleth her bridegroom

At Beltane, the evidence of new life is everywhere. The trees are hung with sweet-smelling blossom. Birds are hatching their eggs. The trees are filled with birdsong. Dandelions and buttercups appear.

Traditional May Day rites from the European traditions are strongly associated with fertility. In pre-Puritan Britain, young men and maidens would go into the woods together on May Eve to gather May

blossoms. 'And,' Puritans noted disapprovingly, 'many would emerge no longer maids.' Rural life was much earthier than life today. Often the bedding would proceed the wedding, not only because young men and women are moved by the same impulses as today, but because in farming communities a man with fertile seed and a fertile wife who could bear children were essential. The work needed many hands and the more children, the more there were to work. Marriage often followed evidence of pregnancy.

Traditional May celebrations involved crowning a May Queen, a young woman of child-bearing age, who would process the village as a symbol of the young Goddess. In Catholic countries there are sometimes similar processions today, but the young woman is under the guise of the Virgin Mary.

Another May Day tradition is May-pole dancing. Whereas the May Queen symbolizes the Goddess, it is the May-pole which symbolizes the God. The ribbons which are woven about the pole by the dancers celebrate the fertility of the God.

Midsummer

(noon)

The God in his power will be king of the land

At Midsummer the crops are growing, flowers blooming and young
have been born to the herds in the fields, but nothing can endure and
blossom forever. The message of the cosmos is change. The days have
lengthened, but soon the shadows will stretch once more.

Midsummer rites in Paganism are often dedicated to the Solar Hero.
There have been many of these in myth and history, and in the
boundary between the two. King Arthur was such a solar hero king. He
fought for the powers of light and right against the forces of
destruction and darkness, but he was a warrior in the service of his
people rather than a fighter for fighting's sake – his sword was raised in
the service of the feminine. The relationship between masculine and
feminine is interwoven in the symbolism of Midsummer. The Sun King
is at the height of his powers in the Northern Hemisphere when the
sun is in the astrological sign of Cancer, ruled by the Moon and most
feminine sign of the Zodiac. The true Solar Hero is therefore one who

knows and honours the feminine within himself and within others.

A Celtic God who can be invoked at Midsummer is the Irish God Lugh, a God of Light. In Irish myth, like many solar heroes, Lugh slays the old king whose reign has become negative. A battle between the God of the old year and the God of the new may form part of Pagan celebrations. The force of life is ever at war with the force of destruction and death. At the Midsummer battle, the young God slays the older God, but often in myths and legends the Solar Hero is wounded and gradually begins to lose his strength. This symbolizes that the days begin to shrink even though summer is still at full height.

Lughnasadh

(mid-afternoon)

The Goddess is weeping, her sickle is stained

Lughnasadh, the Games of Lugh, is the Irish name given to the festival of 1 August. It is also known by its Saxon name of *Lammas*, Loaf Mass. The loaf is the first loaf baked from the newly-gathered corn, for Lammas celebrates the corn harvest. Once the corn was safely gathered, there would be time for general rejoicing and people could cease work for a few days and enjoy a well-earned rest. Lugh's Games were celebrated with fairs, contests and revels.

   Yet death is present in many ways at Lammas. The food of life comes from a plant baked dry by the Sun, which now begins to fade in strength. The fields of ripened corn are also home to foxes, rabbits and other small creatures of the field. As the reapers cut their circular swathe from the outer edge of the fields to the inner, the animals are trapped at the centre. Around the edge, humans with cudgels wait for them to break their cover and attempt to flee. Usually they fail and there is meat for the pot, but also blood upon the corn; in the midst of Summer Sun and the grain of life is the blood of death. In fields of the past this reminder was present throughout the growing season. Untainted by chemical sprays, red poppies bloomed amongst the corn. This reminder is important, for Paganism does not romanticize Nature. The cycle of the seasonal festivals is a wheel, ever turning and moving onwards. If we understand this in our own lives, then we adapt and change. We take each day as a gift which is all the more precious because it is transient and we learn to extract hope, peace and joy from a draught which is inevitably mixed with bitterness.

The Goddess celebrated at Lammas is the bountiful Mother, but she is also the Crone, wielder of the sickle. Lammas is therefore a time of feminine transition. Its themes are about letting go and moving onwards in our life's journey.

Autumn/Fall Equinox

(sunset)

The roses are dead and the birds have gone
and the rain has washed away the Sun

The Autumn or Fall Equinox, like Lammas, is often celebrated as a harvest festival, this time for the remainder of the crops. At the Equinox, however, the approach of the cold of winter is noticeable and our orientation changes from outwards and long sunny days outside to inside, inwards and the long dark nights.

Related to autumn are myths which explain the onset of winter and the disappearance of seasonal greenery. One of the best known of these is the myth of the Greek Goddess Demeter and her daughter Kore, who is also known as Persephone. Kore is stolen away by Hades, Lord of the Underworld, who wants her for his bride. Demeter is distraught and goes in search of her daughter. She blasts the land in her wrath and Nature begins to die. Eventually she discovers Hades' wrong-doing and has him summoned to Mount Olympus, the home of the Gods, for judgement. The judgement of the Gods is that Kore's time must be divided between her mother's realm of Earth and her husband's realm of the Underworld. For two thirds of the year, she will roam the Earth and Nature will grow. For the remainder, she will be beneath the Earth and this will be winter. This period corresponds roughly to the period between the Equinox and Imbolc when Kore reappears once more to renew the land. Pagan celebrations may take the form of a mystery play to enact the story of Demeter and Kore.

Another theme inherent in the Equinox is the equality between the hours of darkness and the hours of light, but here it is darkness which is in the ascendant. A good time for celebrations is therefore sunset, for we are entering the darker time of the year.

Autumn is also associated with turning inwards in another sense. The Equinox tides and winds may bring storm and are considered in Paganism to be a time of transition. This is apparent in the world of Nature. Leaves fall from the trees, birds migrate, the signs of life disappear one by one. The Mystery Initiations of Eleusis in Greece took place at this time and for those of us on a spiritual path it can be a good time to turn inwards and renew our own dedication to our chosen path. Some Pagan groups practise mystery initiation rites which are designed to show through symbol and enactment important messages about the meaning of life and death.

Samhain/Hallowe'en

In the dark of the night, the ancestors walk

Most people will be more familiar with Samhain than with some of the other Pagan festivals because of customs associated with Hallowe'en. At Samhain we know that we are entering winter and indeed its Celtic name meant Summer's End. Winter brought snow and frost and meant that only a few animals would have enough grass to graze and fodder for their indoor feeding. Many animals had to be slaughtered and their meat salted for the winter. Samhain was therefore associated with death in a very real way. It also had death associations for other reasons. With the onset of cold, the death rate would go up, something which is still true today. Samhain was therefore treated as a festival of the dead, a time for remembering those who had gone before.

Our Celtic ancestors had great reverence for the head, which was considered the seat of inspiration and learning. Heads of worthy opponents would be cut off and taken back to display in the communal hall. This may seem barbaric to Pagans today, but our ancestors' lives were harsher and rawer than our own and they did not share our physical squeamishness. Remnants of the veneration of the head are found at Samhain in the custom of hollowing out pumpkins, carving faces in them and placing candles inside them to light the Samhain feast.

Other customs reflect the desire to commune at this time with the ancestors. Often an extra place would be set at the feast and food left out all night for dead relatives who might come and visit during Samhain night.

Samhain is a time of coming to terms with death, something which many of us find very difficult. This may not be the death of the body, but of other things which we have lost during the year – relationships, jobs, material wealth. Samhain takes place during the astrological sign of Scorpio, which is ruled by the element of Water and especially the sea. Water transforms and changes. It washes away pain and sadness and Samhain is a good time to meditate on letting go of past hurts and wrongs.

Yule

The Winter Solstice marks an important transition and one which was eagerly awaited by our ancestors. The Solstice is the nadir of the year, its lowest point in terms of daylight and energy, after which the year begins to turn.

Many Christmas customs are adapted from Paganism – the bringing in of a special Yule log, feasting, games and celebration. Bringing an evergreen tree into the house and decorating it is also a Pagan custom. Amongst the bare and skeletal deciduous trees, the evergreen stands as a sign of hope that spring will one day return to the land; so too the bright red berried holly. Pagans also give gifts at Yule.

The word 'Yule' comes from the Germanic languages and was to our Germanic ancestors what the feast of Samhain was to the Celts. It was a time for gathering in the communal hall, of eating and drinking; a time to listen to stories; a time to sing of adventure and of love.

Many Pagans celebrate the birth of the Sun Child, who will mature and become the young God of Spring. This time of year was celebrated as the birth of the Sun Child long before Christianity, which later adopted it as a matter of convenience for the birth date of its own God. The emphasis in Pagan Yule celebrations, however, is not only on the

Sun Child but also on his Mother, the Great Mother Goddess who brings new life and hope to the land.

The seasonal festivals of Paganism have a very important message: that the Wheel of the Year turns from darkness to light and back to darkness again; from ploughing, sowing, growth, fruition, reaping, harvest, sleeping, renewal to ploughing again. Our individual lives and destinies come and go, but the life force itself endures, remanifests and moves on.

Spiritual Practice

The purpose of spiritual practice is to draw nearer the Gods, the Divine source of all things. Two ways of doing this are through developing a sense of Sacred Time and Sacred Place.

Sacred time

Celebrating the seasonal cycle is one way of creating Sacred Time. We can also create Sacred Time on a daily, weekly or monthly basis by setting aside time which is not devoted to maintaining our physical bodies, earning our living, caring for families, developing our intellects through study or our physical prowess through sport. It is setting aside time to honour the Divine force which gives life to the universe.

When people think of someone as 'religious', they often mean that he or she visits a place of communal worship – a church, synagogue, mosque or temple. Communal worship is not essential in Paganism. If the Divine is everywhere, including within ourselves, we do not have to go out to meet it; nor do we need to share our religious expression with others. Pagans may choose to observe Sacred Time with others or they may not. The choice is an individual one.

We may set aside Sacred Time in many ways. In most spiritual systems, there is some form of observance at the beginning and end of each day and sometimes at special times throughout the day as well. Observance is a matter of individual choice in Paganism. Some Pagans

meditate at the beginning and/or end of each day. This may be done indoors or outdoors. Pagans who see their Deities not as separate beings but as different expressions of the Divine Unity and Pantheistic Pagans who see the Divine in All tend to speak of meditating on or communing with the Divine. This may involve contemplating a particular God or Goddess image in order to come to an understanding of what this aspect of the Divine means in our own lives. Meditation can, however, be much more abstract and involve emptying the mind of thought, stilling the busy byways of consciousness and entering a state of interior stillness in which the boundaries of self and other are dissolved.

Some Pagans pray. Again this may take place either indoors or out doors. Polytheistic Pagans see different Gods as personages dwelling in another realm. Their approach to their Deities is not so different from how a monotheist (someone who believes there is only one true God) might see his or her God, except that a Pagan might pray to a number of Deities.

Other Pagans may simply have a place in their garden they visit each day to remind themselves of who and what they are and of their place in the universe.

Honouring the day by simple words of welcome is another powerful way of linking ourselves with the greater universe and reminding ourselves that we are not alone in it. It is part of us and we of it. This welcome may be a simple phrase:

Hail to thee, O Sun, in thy rising,
thou comest forth in beauty, O my Lady of Light

or our greeting may be wordless. Observance of Sacred Time may be as simple as someone coming home from the end of a day's work, washing, lighting a candle on his or her altar, entering for a few moments into the interior stillness of meditation, then extinguishing the light and making the children's supper. What those few moments will have given us, brief though they may be, is a reminder that despite the frenzy of the world around us, there is within us a place of peace and harmony which is a reflection of the deeper peace and harmony of the Divine. Another way to help us focus our lives is to keep a personal journal in which we reflect upon our lives at the end of each day.

Many people have irregular and hectic lives. This makes daily spiritual practice difficult. Another approach is to set aside blocks of time for vigils, retreats or vision quests. Vigils, long periods spent in meditation at a selected spot, can be an important way of overcoming our habits of thought and opening ourselves to new inspiration.

Vision quests, which involve fasting and spending time outside in a Sacred Place, are common in many Pagan cultures. These help us separate ourselves for a time from our everyday concerns to focus on what is really important – our inner spirit which is eternal and enduring. Retreats in Pagan, non-denominational or ecumenical settings can also help renew the wellsprings of our spirituality. Meeting with others of like mind but from different spiritual paths can be a source of great joy. They help us see that although our religions may be superficially differ-ent we are all seeking in our own ways to know the Divine.

Sacred place

To Pagans, all the Earth is sacred, but certain places have always been seen as holy places, where the veil between this world and the Otherworld is thin. Our ancestors thought particular spots had a *genius loci*, a spirit of the place. This can be thought of either as a particular atmosphere which the place invokes, or as a personality or entity. The landscape of Europe contains holy wells, sacred mountains, mysterious standing stones and earth barrows, many of whose purposes we can only guess. Similar sacred sites, power points, places of pilgrimage and burial grounds are found across the landscape of North America, Australia and other countries.

Sometimes these sacred sites are natural formations. Places where two elements meet are often considered particularly sacred – high mountains where earth meets air, the place between sea and shore, springs which emerge from deep beneath the earth, waterfalls which cascade through the air, caves which go deep into the earth. Other places evoke a sense of wildness – woodlands where few humans go, moorlands swept by the power of wind, and the great sea.

Trees and groves were particularly sacred to our ancestors and one of the first acts of Christian missionaries was to chop down the sacred groves of those they were seeking to convert from their Pagan Deities. Trees have always been evocative to those who see the Divine as manifest in Nature. Trees outlive human beings. Indeed, some trees, such as the great sequoia trees of California, are older than Christianity. Trees represent continuity, endurance and wisdom. Deciduous trees are living images of the seasonal cycle of death, rest, reawakening and renewal and are therefore symbols of hope.

Trees are also important to us in a very practical way. They are the lungs of our planet and maintain the oxygen in our atmosphere. While our ancestors may not have understood all the ins and outs of the biological cycle, on an intuitive level they understood much better than we trees' importance.

There are many ways in which we can gain a sense of Sacred Place. We can choose a Sacred Place and visit it each festival to see how it changes with the seasons. Alternatively, we can choose eight different places, one for each festival.

Your Sacred Place might be an ancient site which has been used by Pagans long ago. It might be a place which is evocative and meaningful for you. Meditate there, picnic, dance or perform a simple ritual. Different festivals have associations with different times of day and exploring sacred sites at different hours can be very rewarding. The site

which seems mundane by day may be powerful and mysterious at night when the tourists have gone home. The site which seems warm and friendly by day may be a strange place indeed at dawn.

Worshipping at ancient sites is something that attracts many Pagans, but care and sensitivity are needed. In North America and Australia, Europeans are recent immigrants. The sacred sites of the land are those of other peoples and we must respect their right to restrict access to them if they wish. In Europe, the Neolithic spirits of a burial mound might not appreciate our holding a full-scale Pagan celebration there. Our midnight drumming, while delightfully evocative to us, might seem no more than a rowdy party.

We must also respect sites on a practical level. If too many people use ancient sites, we will damage them. If we use woodland for our rites, we should be careful that we do not damage trees. (I have seen urban Pagans building a ritual fire next to the trunk of an ancient oak.) We must also take home with us our urban litter.

Get to know your local environment

Connecting with the Divine in Nature is not only a spiritual exercise. Most of us know little about our locality or the other life forms which inhabit it. How many of us can recognize its trees, birds, wild animals, flowers and herbs? There is a language which tells us about natural cycles, but we have forgotten it. If we learn to recognize the birds in our fields, woods, parks and gardens, we will get to know their seasonal migrations. We will learn to recognize by the birds' early departure if winter is to be harsh. If we learn to look at clouds and to register the direction of the wind, we will know when rain is coming, when we are likely to get a storm. This is no longer essential knowledge as it was when humans were dependent on farming, fishing and hunting for their livelihood, but when we are ignorant we walk about in a kind of blindness. A return to Paganism is a return to seeing.

It is not only visiting Sacred Places which is important, but also getting there. Walking to sacred sites or pilgrimage is an important part of all religious traditions. To walk along an ancient path to a sacred site is to walk a way that generations and generations have walked before with a spiritual purpose in mind. These energies will be imprinted upon the landscape and, in tuning into these patterns, we tune into the sense of reverence of those who have gone before.

Walking the land is one way of 'reconnecting'. Another is living on it or from it. Many Pagan rituals and events take place outside and in summer in active Pagan countries there are camps which enable us to live close to Nature for a while. Often there are opportunities to learn ancient crafts or tend crops. This does not mean

that Pagans wish to return to a full-time life of self-sufficiency (though some do), but such skills are empowering. We may not all want to live off the land, but growing some of our own food – even if it is only tomatoes or herbs in a window box – enables us to reconnect with the cycles of growth in Nature.

It is not only the daylight world we need to know, but also the world of night. Above our heads in the night sky is a universe of myriad beauty, filled with planets, stars, shooting stars – all signs that life exists beyond our world. The night sky opens us to worlds of wonder even with the naked eye. With a small telescope we can see a universe of incredible beauty.

It was by turning their minds, hearts and spirits to these outer things that our ancestors learned to love and cherish the universe in which they had been born. If we close our eyes to the beauty of the night, we lose a window into a wider world which shows us that humanity's place in it is small. Strangely enough, this is not threatening, but humbling and joyful. When we are beset by our own problems and concerns, looking outwards and seeing the reality of their smallness allows us to stand back; to see things in perspective; to understand that all things pass and so too will anxiety, pain and fear. By looking outward, we rekindle our hope.

Local customs

Within the traditional calendar of all countries are customs and ceremonies of Pagan origin. Some of these have fallen into disuse except in rural areas, but one way of renewing our Paganism is to revive traditional customs. These do not have to be reserved exclusively for Pagans. There are many customs which the whole community can enjoy and which make valuable links between people of different beliefs, both spiritual and secular. If you look in books of local folklore, you will find customs such as May celebrations, well-dressing, times when sacred hills and sites would be visited. Schools and other community organizations can often be persuaded to help revive these. They are all useful ways for people to be introduced to Pagan ideas, reminding us of our relationship to our environment and, equally importantly, binding communities together in a highly mobile age when we are not all closely related, working for a common employer, long-standing residents of our localities or sharing a common religion. Many who see themselves as being of other faiths or of no faith at all find meaning in reconnecting themselves with the place they live and in shared communal activity.

Creative Paganism

Ancient theatre derived from religious ceremonies and mystery plays is designed to help us understand our relationships to the Gods and to the wider universe. In Eastern societies, festivals with dragons, performers dressed as mythological figures, and plays which illustrate mythological and religious themes are all very familiar.

Today, there has been a great revival through performance art of ritual theatre and it is now part of the syllabus in many drama schools. Ritual theatre has also become important in the Pagan community, as Pagans have started to meet in large outdoor gatherings. Wordy rites are of little use in a field full of thousands of people, so there has been a return to ritual processions and the use of evocative symbols such as giants, wicker men, fire mazes, dance, drumming, music and chanting as a way of unifying Pagans in celebration and honouring the Gods.

Other ways of representing archetypal themes are through games. Tugs of war between summer and winter express in living symbol the dynamic of growth and decay which we celebrate in our seasonal cycle. Egg hunts for children illustrate the return of fertility to the land. Folk dances evoke many of the themes of life and death. Many of these are present in Morris dancing, particularly in what is known as Bedlam or Black Morris, where the participants black their faces and are dressed in the colourful rags of mummers. Creative participation is a way of taking the messages of Paganism back to where they belong – to the people – so that all can access them at the level they wish.

The arts are involved in Paganism in other ways. Many forms of Paganism focus on developing creativity as a way of celebrating our spirituality and of increasing and enhancing it. Creating poetry, plays, ritual prose, songs, chants, music and dance to honour the Gods helps us engage in our celebrations, so that they are not performances by others, but something to which we contribute our energy and power.

Rites in Pagan life

All the more organized forms of Paganism involve group ritual. Ritual is also a feature of non-aligned Pagan groups. Four major types of ritual are found in Paganism:

- *Observances of Sacred Time*: the celebrations of the seasonal cycle and in some traditions Full and possibly New Moon celebrations
- *Rites of passage to mark transitions* in the life cycle – birth, maturity, marriage, giving birth, ageing and death
- *Initiation rituals* which take adult initiates into closer understanding of the Divine Mysteries
- *Rituals for specific intentions* – healing rituals, eco-magic rituals to enlist the aid of the Gods in protecting the environment

Sacred space

Pagans are creative and spontaneous in the way they honour their Gods and rites vary between the traditions. However, there are some typical patterns. Pagan rites may take place anywhere. They are not confined to a particular building designated as a church. Often, Pagans prefer not to celebrate their rites indoors, but instead to find a quiet place outside beneath the open sky and with their feet upon the earth. Often Pagan ritual takes place in woods and fields. Some Pagans will create a space in their gardens for their rites. Perhaps they will plant a circle of trees or mark the space with a circle of stones. Venerating the Divine outside in the world of Nature is important because Nature is the mirror of the Divine. In the pattern of the seasons, we see the ever-renewing and ever-changing life force and in attuning ourselves to the seasonal cycle around us, we can come to an under standing of the greater cosmos.

Outdoor ritual is not always practical and rites may take place in Pagans' own homes. A special room may be set aside or there may be a small shrine in the corner of bedroom or living-room. Some may have a statue of a Goddess or God on their altar. These may be beautiful and humanoid images such as those of ancient Greece and Rome, but they may be much simpler – a rounded rock which is suggestive of a pregnant woman, a piece of bark which appears to have eyes as though the Green Man himself were looking out through them. Some Pagans keep symbols of the Four Elements on their altars – a candle for Fire, incense for Air, a bowl of water for Water and rock, crystal or a bowl of earth for Earth. Other objects of natural beauty may be added to remind us of the natural world around us – flowers, a plant, a feather, a shell. Pagans do not worship these objects, or indeed statues of the Gods. Their role is to remind us of the Divinity which lies beyond them.

Creating sacred space

Group ritual often takes place in a circle or square with a central altar or fire. If you think about the layout of Christian churches, you will realize that this is different from the Sacred Space which has been used in the West over the past millennium or so. Churches were built as rectangles with God at one end and human beings at the other. In Pagan rites, the Divine force is seen as being at the centre. This is not only the centre of the group of worshippers but also the centre of ourselves, for Pagans believe that each of us is at our core Divine. Each of us is also part of the priesthood – if that is our wish. We can create our own rites and forms of worship and have no need of priestly hierarchy to authorize and sanction them.

Circular rites are common in Goddess groups and in WiseCraft, where magic may be part of the rites. The circle is thought of as a container for magical energy which is raised within the circle and which must be focused and contained before it is 'sent' to do its work. But not all Pagan rites are carried out in circular space. Rites for the veneration of Deities do not necessarily need this type of space, though many use it.

Entry to Sacred Space may be marked in a number of ways. Some traditions wear special dress or robes. Others remove their shoes or if

outside wear special sandals. Watches are usually removed, for Sacred Space is considered to be outside the laws of human measured time and time should not be a preoccupation within it.

Often the boundaries of Sacred Space are marked out to signify that the space has been set apart. They may be physical if a circle of stones has been made or if the rite takes place in a room specially set aside for worship, but often the boundaries will be marked by drawing a circle around the space with a staff or ritual knife or sword, either symbolically in the air or physically on the ground.

There may be a ceremonial procession of the Four Elements – sprinkling the boundaries with water to which salt (considered a symbol of the element of Earth) has been added, censing them and bearing light or fire around them. Air, Fire, Water and Earth are thought of as energy in different forms, from the least to the most solid. These four symbols represent the whole of material creation. In Nature the elements are seen as the air we breathe, the Sun which warms us, the waters of which our bodies are mainly comprised and the earth which produces the bounty which nourishes us. These are the forces necessary for life and are therefore honoured.

Most Western Paganism, like Native American and other indigenous traditions, honours the sacred directions of East, South, West and North. This is a symbolic way of honouring the land around us. The quarters are often thought of as Gateways which allow communion with different aspects of the spiritual realm. In Western Paganism, the Four Directions are associated with the Four Elements: Air in the East, Fire in the South, Water in the West, Earth in the North. By addressing the Four Directions, we are symbolically addressing the whole of existence. The ceremonial salutation may take place by taking a symbol of the element to the appropriate quarter and invoking the presence of the Elemental powers to protect the Sacred Space.

The circle guarded by the Four Quarters is symbolized by the circle-cross and appears in the symbolism of many Pagan peoples.

Addressing the Gods

Once Sacred Space has been created, the Gods are addressed in a form appropriate to the Tradition. Some Traditions practise invocation – an individual enters a state of trance and incarnates the Deity for the duration of the rite. In Western Paganism, incarnation of the Deity tends to be practised more by Pagans who see their Gods as different aspects of the Divine force and as communication links between humanity and the Divine.

The invocation of the Gods may be followed by enactment of a seasonal myth, by rites of passage, or by specific prayers or magic to achieve particular ends, such as healing for individuals or for the land.

Not all Pagans practise magic and for many this holds no appeal. The very word is strange in our modern society. Magic as practised by Pagans involves uniting the minds of a group to a common purpose and visualizing that coming about by an act of focused will. The rationale of magic is too complex to explain here, but recent advances in science and our understanding of morphogenetic fields lend more rather than less credit to some of the magical ideas of so-called primitive peoples.

Community
rites of passage

Most of us wish to mark important life occasions – the birth of a child, marriage, death – through community celebration and the calling down of a blessing from the Gods. Pagans may also celebrate other rites which would be familiar to a tribal society, but which have not been so widely observed in the modern world – the transition from adolescence to adulthood for instance.

Pagans do not necessarily call upon a more experienced member of the community to perform their rites of passage. Many parents will arrange their own naming ceremonies for their children. Pagans who are marrying, or handfasting, as it is often called, may choose to conduct much of the rite themselves. Conducting our own funerals is somewhat tricky and here an experienced community member is likely to be called on.

In Paganism, rites of passage are seen as times of celebration and joy. This may seem strange in connection with funeral rites, but the emphasis in Pagan funerals is on honouring the person who has departed from us, but also on celebrating his or her life and achievements and celebrating his or her entry into the Otherworld.

Most Pagan rites will end with the sharing of wine, beer or mead and either token food in the form of bread or specially baked cakes, or a full-scale feast. Feasting is more likely to form part of seasonal celebrations and will involve traditional foods appropriate to the season. The feast is not considered a lesser part of the celebration, but an equally important one. It is a way of enjoying the bounty of the Gods and of sharing it with others.

If Pagan's practices resonate with you, how can you find out more?

Useful Addresses/ Further Reading

This book does not pretend to offer any more than a brief glimpse of the richness of modern Paganism. If you wish to explore further, there are books which can help you understand Paganism more deeply. If you want to go beyond reading to a more active involvement, you are recommended to contact one of the many Pagan organizations. Those listed here are the larger organizations which have been running for some time. They can also facilitate contact with more local groups and those following a particular Pagan tradition.

Large Pagan Organizations/Main Journals

UK and Europe

The Pagan Federation,
BM Box 7097,
London WC1N 3XX,
UK; Fax: 01691 671066,
is the main Pagan group in Europe. The Pagan Federation is a democratic organization run by its voting members. It has an annual conference in London, regional conferences, local group meetings and contacts world-wide. It publishes *Pagan Dawn*, an informative quarterly journal, and has a useful information pack on modern European Paganism and a Wicca information pack. Pagan books can be bought through mail order. Part of the work of the Pagan Federation is to counter prejudice

against Pagans and to provide accurate information on Paganism to government bodies, the media and the general public.

North America

Circle,
PO Box 219,
Mount Horeb,
WI 53572, USA,

organizes Pagan events, fosters contacts, and publishes *Circle Network News*, an informative journal of Nature Spirituality. Circle publishes *The Circle Guide to Pagan Groups* which lists groups in North America and can supply books by mail order. There are gatherings, a land sanctuary, counselling service and many other activities.

Australia and New Zealand

Pan-Pacific Pagan Alliance,
PO Box A486,
Sydney South,
NSW 2000,
Australia,

is the organization for all branches of Paganism in Australia and New Zealand. Its members' magazine lists groups and contacts and the PPPA can advise on Pagan matters generally.

Further Reading

- *Drawing Down the Moon: Witches, Druids, Goddess-Worshippers and other Pagans in America Today*, Margot Adler, Penguin, New York and London, 1997. An excellent survey of North American Paganism with extensive lists of organizations and magazines.

- *Phoenix from the Flame: Living as a Pagan in the twenty-first century*, Vivianne Crowley, Thorsons, London, 1996. Describes in more depth than is possible in this book the origins of the major Western Pagan traditions and the philosophy of Western Paganism.

- *Celtic Wisdom: Seasonal Rituals and Festivals*, Vivianne Crowley, Thorsons, London, 1998. A guide to celebrating the seasonal festivals of Paganism.

- *Listening People, Speaking Earth: Contemporary Paganism*, Graham Harvey, Hurst & Co., London, 1997. Interesting overview of modern Paganism by academic.

- *Nature Religion Today: Paganism in the Modern World*, Joanne Pearson, Richard H. Roberts and Geoffrey Samuels eds., Edinburgh University Press, 1998. Papers from important academic conference on Nature Religion and Paganism.

- *The Triumph of the Moon: A History of Modern Pagan Witchcraft*, Ronald Hutton, Oxford University Press, Oxford, 1999. The first history of modern Wicca.

- *A History of Pagan Europe*, Prudence Jones and Nigel Pennick, Routledge, London, 1995. A history of Western Paganism from ancient times to today.